Embracing *Your New* Normal

A 21 Day Devotional to Support
And Encourage You as You Keep Living

Teraleen R. Campbell

Embracing Your New Normal: A 21 Day Devotional to Support and Encourage You as You Keep Living©
Copyright 2020 by Teraleen R. Campbell

ALL RIGHTS RESERVED. No part of this book may be reproduced in any written, electronic, recording, or photocopying without written permission of the publisher or author. The exception would be in the case of brief quotations embodied in the critical articles or reviews and pages where permission is specifically granted by the publisher or author.

www.teraleencampbell.com

PUBLISHED BY: Pen Legacy® (penlegacy.com)
EDITING/TYPESETTING BY: Carla M. Dean, U Can Mark My Word
COVER DESIGN BY: Christian Cuan

Scripture taken from the New King James Version®. Copyright © 1982 by Thomas Nelson. Used by permission. All rights reserved.

Scripture quotations taken from The Holy Bible, New International Version® NIV® Copyright © 1973 1978 1984 2011 by Biblica, Inc. TM Used by permission. All rights reserved worldwide.

Scripture quotations marked (NLT) are taken from the Holy Bible, New Living Translation, copyright © 1996, 2004, 2007, 2013, 2015 by Tyndale House Foundation. Used by permission of Tyndale House Publishers, Inc., Carol Stream, Illinois 60188. All rights reserved.

Library of Congress Cataloging – in- Publication Data has been applied for.

ISBN: 978-1-7348278-3-5

PRINTED IN THE UNITED STATES OF AMERICA

For bulk orders of 15 or more books, please send an email to teracam@msn.com.

Embracing *Your New* Normal

Dedications

This book is dedicated to the memory of my beloved mother, Cynthia Moses McGregor. It serves as a follow-up to my first book, From Carefree to Caregiver, wherein I chronicled and honored the final years of our journey together. I thank the Lord for selecting me to be my mother's daughter. I am ever mindful of the fact that I am the beneficiary of her prayers.

I also dedicate this to every person who has lost a parent, especially a mother. Please know that I am praying for you. May the pages of this book cause you to be lifted and renewed as you journey on knowing that you are not alone.

Journaling has been a great source of refuge and strength along my quest to embrace my new normal. Therefore, I have included pages for you to journal or take notes after each passage. I encourage you to take advantage of the space. You will find recording your feelings and thoughts to be beneficial to your emotional and spiritual well-being.

What Does It Mean to Embrace Your New Normal?

Since experiencing the transition of my mother, I would say the new normal equals change. It is embracing the change we never prepared for. It is embracing the change we do not feel equipped for. It is accepting change we never asked for. Quite honestly, it is change we do not want.

It is embracing a change that is necessary. Yes, necessary change. It is also what many of us know in our heart of hearts that our loved one would want us to do. They would want us to keep living and move forward with our lives. Therein we are embracing our new normal.

Table of Contents

I Knew	11
Today's Agenda	15
Rest	21
Uncertainty	25
In Her Honor	29
A Shift – New Dynamic	33
One More Day	37
The First Without Her	41
What's Next?	45
The Hardest Day	49
Resilience	55
Race Run	59
Race Run, Part Two	63
I Didn't Know My Own Strength	69
No Fear	73
A Day in the Pit	77
I Still Give Thanks	81
Help Yourself During The Holiday Season	85
Family Matters	89
Christmas	93
You Better Recognize	97
Bonus Chapters:	
Change	103
Not a Day Goes By	107

I Knew...

One of the most difficult aspects of loving someone is letting them go. In this case, it was letting go and allowing my mother to depart from this life.

The truth of the matter is, months before her passing away, God showed me that my mother's departure from this earthly life was imminent. I just didn't know when it would happen. I saw it in a vision; the Lord let me know that He was preparing me for her departure. It was one of the most painful revelations God has ever shared with me, and therefore, I told no one. It was so unsettling. Then, one day, an evangelist messaged me and confirmed what I had already felt in my spirit. She went on to tell me that the Lord said I had served my mother well and that I was going to be alright, although some days I don't feel alright.

After Christmas 2016, my mother became depressed and began to slip further into depression after her mobility declined. Even during her illness, my mother always worked her way back to a level of self-sufficiency. She was able to get in and out of her bed without using the Hoyer lift. She had been able to get in and out of her wheelchair with assistance from an aide, of course. She had even gotten to the point where she could take steps while using her walker. Losing that mobility and becoming reliant on the nursing home staff again was demoralizing to my mother; she felt defeated. I recognized it. However, I could do nothing to change the situation.

It got to the point where my prayers shifted. I asked God if He wasn't going to heal her, then to take her home with Him. Seeing her sink into an abyss was too painful for me. No longer was she the vibrant, positive, joyful mommy who I once knew. She was merely existing. She was not as social. She stayed in her room more, whereas previously, she went to the dining room to socialize with her friends while eating. She used to love going to the rooms of those who were bedridden to offer prayer and encouragement. However, those visits stopped.

By the time her birthday came, she was hardly eating. My family had a ritual of gathering to celebrate Mom's special day. I would pick up red velvet cupcakes and balloons, and we would sing to her in celebration. Long-distance family members usually sent her flowers. This year was different; she barely ate one cupcake. I cried inside. I thank the Lord for the warning, though. Moreover, I thank Him for seeing me through the days when that vision became my painful reality.

Scripture

Trust in the LORD with all your heart and lean not on your own understanding; ^{6}In all your ways acknowledge Him, and He shall direct your paths.

~ **Proverbs 3:5-6 NKJV**

Prayer

Father, thank you for trusting me with sensitive information. Sometimes, however, I wish you didn't trust me so much. This is painful! As I write through my tears, I can only say that I am leaning, depending, and trusting you to see me through. I cannot make it without you. Amen!

Embracing Your New Normal

Notes:

_____
_____
_____
_____
_____
_____
_____
_____
_____
_____
_____

Teraleen R. Campbell

Today's Agenda

Planning funerals is not something most of us purposely learn to do. However, I must say the process of helping countless others plan these events while being there for them during their time of loss proved to be beneficial during my time of need. Those experiences prepared me for one of the saddest, yet most meaningful events of my life–my mother's celebration of life. What I realized was the specific tasks (creating the program, selecting an appropriate outfit, picking songs, selecting a eulogist, etc.) were the easy part. In reality, I was unprepared for what felt like a door slammed in my face as a result of emotions that hit me so incredibly hard and left me feeling overwhelmed. I remember at the time thinking to myself, *This is really happening.*

I can recall the morning of my mother's funeral. Being the task-oriented person that I am, I woke up and told myself that the only thing on that day's agenda was to bury my mother. (Insert tears) At that moment, I wished my brain didn't function the way it does. Who else thinks like this? (sigh) Alas, I was able to put together enough coherent words to pray. I asked the Lord to carry me through that dreadful day. It was a day I had never imagined and one I never wanted to live through again.

I digress, one thing I truly appreciate is the fact that my mother had her financial matters in order before leaving this earth. To be blunt, she had sufficient life insurance. Because she had an active life insurance policy, we did not have to worry about covering her funeral expenses. Additionally, after her health started to decline, I established a pre-need burial plan. By doing so, I put a significant down payment on a grave plot at the cemetery and made regular payments toward it. While not completely paid off, I did not have the stress of having to figure out how to send my mother off in a manner that would be worthy of the life she had lived.

In retrospect, I realize God will hold us up, even during the days when we feel ill-equipped. I know for a fact that He carried me through that day, allowing me to check every item on my to-do list in such a manner that my mother's homegoing service was glorious and fitting for the queen who we had just lost.

I realized there would be days when I will have to face less than desirable tasks and action items. Seeing how God got me through that most difficult time makes me more confident in His ability to carry me through in the future.

I am reminded of an old song: Ask the Savior to help you, comfort, strengthen, and keep you. He is willing to aid you. Jesus will carry you through.

Thank you, Lord, for carrying me through the days when my agenda and to-do list is overwhelming.

Scripture

For I, the LORD your God, will hold your right hand, saying to you, 'Fear not, I will help you.'

~ Isaiah 41:13 NKJV

God is my savior; I will trust him and not be afraid. The Lord gives me power and strength; he is my savior.

~ Isaiah 12:2 GNT

Prayer

While I do appreciate the way, my brain is wired to process information, this is not one of them. In fact, it has made this situation more painful. Oh Lord, how I wish that I were able to process this differently. At the same time, Father, I appreciate you for sending me help in human form as well as through your spirit. I ask that you continue to help me. You blessed me with the ability to think logically and process information. I am so grateful to have an advocate in you. Amen!

Embracing Your New Normal

Notes:

Teraleen R. Campbell

Rest

The day after my mother's homegoing service, all I wanted to do was sleep. Instead, I got up and went to church with my family because I know that's what Mom would have wanted me to do. I spent the day with my cousins who had come to town for the funeral. We had Sunday dinner together, eating the banquet-sized leftovers from the repast that the church had sent to the house.

That Monday was Memorial Day, and I was supposed to return to work on Tuesday. However, when I woke up early that Tuesday morning, everything in me was exhausted. I could not muster the strength to brush my teeth, let alone leave the house and go to the office. So, I called my boss and told him that I needed another day. He was so gracious and understanding, telling me that he hadn't expected me to return so soon. He then reminded me that I had plenty of paid leave to use. After hearing that, I breathed a sigh of relief and rolled over to go back to sleep.

I had been running on adrenaline for nearly a month. It began when my mother went into the hospital for what would turn out to be the last time. I had gotten a call from the nursing home while I was at work. Thankfully, two of my close friends dropped everything and made the two-hour trip with me. It continued through Mother's Day weekend when my best friend and I spent the weekend in ICU with Mom. I asked the Lord to give me at least one more Mother's Day with her, even if she was not in the best of health. Most of all, I did not want her to die on Mother's Day itself. The Lord granted both of my requests, and for that, I am grateful.

Mom was placed in hospice that final weekend, and it was surreal signing those hospice forms. I am thankful my family and close friends were there for me because I felt as though I had been on a rollercoaster that was steadily going downhill.

The funeral was the climax of the post-death experience for me. It was a glorious homegoing service full of praise, just as my mother would have wanted, and the church was near capacity. Then, there I was two days later faced with my new reality, and it left me drained. For once, I decided to listen to my body and rest.

Scripture

In peace I will lie down and sleep, for you alone, O LORD, will keep me safe.

~ Psalm 4:8 NLT

Prayer

Lord, today I ask that you grant me sweet rest. Give me rest on those nights when my spirit is unsettled. I do my best to cast the cares of this new reality upon you. Help me to listen both to your Holy Spirit and to my body. As I must go on, I recognize the need to make sure I rest my mind, body, and spirit. I thank you in advance. In Jesus' name, Amen

Embracing Your New Normal

Notes:

Teraleen R. Campbell

Uncertainty

Walking through a new normal means that we will be confronted with uncertainty. There will be uncertain times and days. There will be instances wherein you second guess yourself and are trying to find direction. There will be times when you find yourself struggling to restore your life's peace and days when you are working to rediscover your passion and purpose. These are normal aspects of the grieving process that can occur when the realization hits you that the person who gave you life is no longer on Earth.

What I have come to learn while navigating through this new normal is that I must pray even more. I have to seek peace and pursue it. Some people will be left by the wayside, but not necessarily because they've done anything wrong or I've done something wrong. Simply put, the new normal might not include them. Therefore, I'm learning not to force that which does not fit, because everything cannot come into this new normal that I am embracing.

The truth is, there will be nights when you cry yourself to sleep because the future seems uncertain, I did. There will be nights when you go to sleep with questions and wake up the next morning with those same questions in your mind. I have done that too. Through those days and nights, my affirmation is simple: Although I may not have the answers, I serve a God who does, and He has never left me hanging. The fact that I am in a covenant relationship with a certain and steady God who has seen me through the most uncertain and unpredictable days is enough to keep me during this season of my life. He will see you through, too!

Scripture
The LORD says, "I will guide you along the best pathway for your life. I will advise you and watch over you."
~ **Psalm 32:8 NLT**

And if God cares so wonderfully for wildflowers that are here today and thrown into the fire tomorrow, he will certainly care for you. Why do you have so little faith?
~ **Matthew 6:30 NLT**

Prayer
Lord, you know what I am dealing with. You know what I am facing. You know how I am feeling. At this moment, I am grateful that I don't have to pour out my heart to you because you already know. I find comfort in the fact that you know, care, and promised to watch over me. I rest in the fact that my uncertainties are certain with you, my God, providing guidance. Thank you for being my covering, in Jesus' name. Amen.

Embracing Your New Normal

Notes:

_____
_____
_____
_____
_____
_____
_____
_____
_____
_____

Teraleen R. Campbell

In Her Honor

Most have no idea of the story behind the glory. For the second time, I participated in the Survivors Rock the Runway segment at the Silent Tears No More Prayer Breakfast, which is held during Domestic Violence Awareness Month. In doing so, I shared my story and strutted in honor of my mother. I did it for the woman who endured and overcame an abusive marriage when I was a teenager. For five years, we both endured verbal abuse and beatings from my stepfather, but God enabled us to go from being victims to victorious! I've come in contact with many young people who have lived in abusive homes and feel as if they have no voice. For this reason, one of my goals is to help children who have been abused or witnessed abuse in their homes, as I did, in hopes that they will break the cycle of domestic violence.

Upon returning home, I thought about the various struggles and challenges that my mother endured during her 67 years of life. Through it all, she never lost her positive outlook and always held fast to her belief that God was her source and her strength. She leaned wholly on the Lord and trusted in Him to see her through. It is that same faith and tenacity that I carry with me, even to this day.

It has only been five months since my mother's transition, and some days have been more challenging than others. However, I've realized that I can embark upon actions that will honor the love and positive outlook that she possessed and instilled into countless others.

Scripture

Honor your father and mother. Then you will live a long, full life in the land the LORD your God is giving you.

~ **Exodus 20:12 NLT**

Prayer

Heavenly Father, I am so grateful you blessed me with a mother who was a light in my life. I thank you that her light not only shined down upon me, but it was visible to others and lifted them, also. Thank you for the example of an overcomer. Because she overcame, I realize that I, too, can overcome. Help me to do things that honor her memory and bring you glory. This is my prayer today. In Jesus' name, Amen.

Embracing Your New Normal

Notes:

_____
_____
_____
_____
_____
_____
_____
_____
_____
_____
_____

Teraleen R. Campbell

A Shift - New Dynamic

On November 29, 2019, the dynamic of my family was permanently altered. That was the day my aunt Josephine departed this earth. After 82 years of life, my aunt was the last member of my mother's generation to pass on to glory.

After a family member transitions, we are not only left with the responsibility to survive but to also carry out the legacy of our grandmother, parents, and other ancestors. Like my mother and grandmother, I seem to be the glue that holds us together. Some members of my family do not know each other. They know each other's names, but that is about it. Bonding and interaction have been limited. Over the past few years, gatherings have occurred primarily when I have been part of coordinating them. I will be honest and admit I am not sure how to continue to carry this load, although it is necessary. I recognize the need to evaluate my level of commitment to see this through.

Sometimes it feels as if the void left as a result of death is too much, and the mere thought is overwhelming to me. On the one hand, it is the feeling of inadequacy. I'm not sure how my mother and grandmother supported everyone while keeping themselves together, but I honestly am not sure that I can fill their shoes. On the other hand, I am not sure I have the desire or bandwidth to handle this load.

Life is very different now. It is more hectic, and personal relationships have taken a hit over the past two decades. I find myself asking the Lord why He gave me this assignment because, quite honestly, I don't want it. Don't get me wrong, I love my family and we get along well when we are together; however, playing the role of family connecter does not appeal to me.

Alas, not my will, but thy will be done, right?

Scripture

And He was withdrawn from them about a stone's throw, and He knelt down and prayed, [42] saying, "Father, if it is Your will, take this cup away from Me; nevertheless not My will, but Yours, be done." [43] Then an angel appeared to Him from heaven, strengthening Him.

~ Luke 22:41-43 NKJV

Prayer

Dear Lord, I admit this is an extremely difficult shift. My family and I need you. Not only do we need you now, but we will need you in the days ahead. We cannot make it without your impartation of strength and courage. We are leaning and trusting in you, knowing that if you help us, we shall be helped. We thank you in advance for helping us to navigate through this new season in our lives. In Jesus' name, Amen.

Embracing Your New Normal

Notes:

_____
_____
_____
_____
_____
_____
_____
_____
_____
_____
_____

Teraleen R. Campbell

One More Day

I am writing this passage while sailing the Caribbean and gazing out at the Atlantic Ocean from the balcony of my cabin. My view is contradictory; it is both extraordinary and uneventful. The crisp, clear blue sky along with the beautiful blue water of the ocean is breathtaking, and there is nothing else in sight besides the sun. The waves ripple as the ship sails through the water.

As I'm sitting on my balcony, something occurred to me. The fact that I can see nothing else in the distance leads to uncertainty and speculation, and I experience a flurry of emotions that nearly brings me to tears.

This is a visual of my life in this new normal; it is uncertain. While I do not know what else is out there, I am confident something is. Then I begin to see faraway objects, although I am unable to distinguish what they are. Likewise, God has more out there for me in this life, and while I cannot see what it is right now, I must continue to trust Him.

Uneventful? Yes, there will be days when I feel as though I am either not progressing or quite frankly stuck. However, just like this plain, yet beautiful blue ocean, the Lord will establish peace in the middle of it. The tranquil sounds of the waves serve as a sign of His peaceful presence.

As I sit on the deck of this mammoth thirteen-story ship, I realize that I've enjoyed my time here, but tomorrow is the day that I must get off the boat and move on. Although we may not feel ready, it is time to disembark from the boat we were once on and cope with this new normal. The boat equals part of our lifestyle. While we are unsure what is out there in the sea of life, we do know that God's got us. He has a plan. Tomorrow is another day, and we must move on. Through it all, He will give us peace and assurance that will enable us to go forth.

Scripture

I am leaving you with a gift—peace of mind and heart. And the peace I give is a gift the world cannot give. So don't be troubled or afraid.

~ John 14:27 NLT

Prayer

Father, I've experienced a flurry of emotions that I cannot adequately articulate. The days have been uncertain, sad, and I'm also a bit afraid. I ask you to help me experience peace and a level of tranquility that only comes from you. Although I thank you for the boat, I also recognize there is life outside of it. Help me, Lord, to gather the strength to move beyond this current space and move forward in you. Help me to move in purpose and continue the legacy. In Jesus' name, Amen.

Notes:

_____
_____
_____
_____
_____
_____
_____
_____
_____
_____
_____

Teraleen R. Campbell

The First Without Her

This month marked my first birthday without my mother. Coming into the month, I experienced some anxiety at the mere thought. So, I stayed in constant prayer, asking the Lord not to allow me to sink into an abyss of depression as I had during the Labor Day holiday.

As the actual day drew closer, a peace that truly surpassed my understanding replaced my apprehension. I still shed some tears, especially the morning of my actual birthday. Lord have mercy, I cried! The reality is, I truly do miss my one and only Mommy.

My mother had this practice of waiting until the afternoon to call me. One year, I thought she had forgotten, so I called and asked if she had forgotten my birthday. She confidently explained that she gave birth to me at 12:15 p.m. Therefore, she did not officially begin celebrating my birth until after that time. We both laughed. I came to expect those afternoon birthday calls. The sad realization that the annual call would not happen this birthday caused a great deal of sadness within me. However, that peace was still in effect. That same peace can be present in your life, also.

Scripture

Now may the Lord of peace himself give you his peace at all times and in every situation. The Lord be with you all.

~ **2 Thessalonians 3:16 NLT**

Prayer

Father, today, I thank you for two things: tears and peace. Although not pleasant, I thank you for the tears because I recognize it is not healthy for me to keep my feelings bottled up inside. Although difficult, you carried me through this day.

I praise you for the ability to acknowledge my feelings, even when they are feelings of sadness. I praise you for peace because that is what I have when everything else seems to fail. I pray that your spirit continues to abide with me. You have been the constant presence in my changing world, for this I am grateful, in Jesus' name. Amen!

Embracing Your New Normal

Notes:

_____
_____
_____
_____
_____
_____
_____
_____
_____
_____
_____

Teraleen R. Campbell

What's Next?

The funeral is over. The phone has stopped ringing; the flowers have wilted, and there are no food deliveries. The visits have also ended, and hardly anyone is around. They were here when I needed them. They have now returned to the normalcy of their lives. Meanwhile, what I once called normal is no more, and I still need them. I am left to face what is commonly known as the new normal. Not only must I face it, but I must ultimately accept and embrace it if I expect to really live again.

I am emotionally and physically tired. My mind is tired, too, as I wonder what's next. Life seems emptier because of the void left after my mother's death. Truthfully, part of me is now gone.

How am I supposed to go on? How do I make it through this? I ask myself, despite people telling me that I will.

While I understand my mother was ready to go home to be with the Lord, the truth is I was not ready for her to leave. Still, I bowed to her will and, ultimately, the will of the almighty God whom she served.

Yes, I know she received the ultimate healing, as they say in church. I do recognize she's not in pain and that her suffering is over. That is the spiritual knowledge kicking in. At the same time, the childlike part of me cries because I want my mommy!! Cindy Moses, my mother, taught me so much. However, she never taught me how to live without her! God has to help me live through this!

Scripture

For we do not have a high priest who is unable to empathize with our weaknesses, but we have one who has been tempted in every way, just as we are—yet he did not sin. ^{16}Let us then approach God's throne of grace with confidence, so that we may receive mercy and find grace to help us in our time of need.

~ Hebrews 4:15-16 NIV

But you, God, see the trouble of the afflicted; you consider their grief and take it in hand. The victims commit themselves to you; you are the helper of the fatherless.

~ Psalm 10:14 NIV

Prayer

Dear Lord, I come to you today in pressing need of your help. I ask that you dispatch ministering angels because I need a special touch from you right now. This burden is too much, and I realize I cannot carry it alone. There is so much on my mind, but I cannot muster the words to articulate my emotions properly. The best thing I can say is that I need you as I face this next season of my life. Amen!

Embracing Your New Normal

Notes:

Teraleen R. Campbell

The Hardest Day

Mother's Day is one of the most difficult days of the year for those whose mothers are no longer living. I became more aware and sensitive to this in 2011. My mother had become seriously ill during the Fall of 2010 due to complications from surgery, which resulted in her being on life support for two months in addition to having to undergo several additional surgeries. As she continued to recover, the medical staff transferred her to a different hospital that specialized in wound care.

I recall going to see her on Mother's Day. I was grateful she was alive, although in a weakened state. At this point, she was unable to feed herself, so I fed her pureed food. She later made a drastic improvement and was able to eat anything she wanted on her own. Thank you, God!

During this particular visit, my mother looked up at one of my closest friends who was with me and asked him about participating in her funeral. Needless to say, I was outdone! I was nearly beside myself; I had no words. Not wanting her to see me fall apart, I quietly slipped out of the room.

The following year as Mother's Day approached, I experienced a heightened awareness of the sensitivity of this day and the impact it has on those who no longer have their mothers. Led to help those who struggle with this holiday, I hosted a prayer call. Having spoken with some close friends and relatives, I had become more aware of how it can affect people in two different ways. For instance, one of my cousins shared with me that for years, she did not allow her children to make plans for her on Mother's Day because she did not view it as a day of celebration, having lost her mother years earlier. Whereas for me, nearly losing my mother made me more sensitive and empathetic towards those who view this day of the year as one of the most difficult.

Since my mother's transition three years ago, I have not physically been able to attend church on Mother's Day. I am not ready. Conversely, I have been very intentional about how I spend the day. I have a very close sistagirl who lost her mother the same week as mine. She and I take a unique approach to Mother's Day; we use the day to celebrate our mothers. We call it Daughter's Day, and instead of mourning our loss, we have repurposed the day to honor their memories and the bond that we shared with them.

For those who view Mother's Day as one of the hardest days, I say, take your time. Know what you can and cannot handle. God understands. He will not condemn you should you decide not to step inside the doors of a church on Mother's Day. He will help you make it through the day. Sometimes that's all you need – to be able to make it through.

Scripture

So many are saying, "God will never rescue him!" ³But you, O LORD, are a shield around me; you are my glory, the one who holds my head high.

~ Psalm 3:2-3 NLT

Embracing Your New Normal

Prayer

Lord, today I thank you for getting me. You understand me. You understand my mood swings – my ups and downs – when others seemingly do not. Moreover, you help me get through. As I approach one of my hardest days, I take time to thank you in advance for helping me. If it were not for you, I would lose it, but you are a consistent helper. I would not make it without you. May this prayer of thanksgiving and adoration affirm my gratefulness to you – my strength, my savior, and my lifter. In Jesus' name, Amen!

Embracing Your New Normal

Notes:

_____
_____
_____
_____
_____
_____
_____
_____
_____
_____
_____

Teraleen R. Campbell

Resilience

Resilience – an ability to recover from or easily adjust to misfortune or change.

Although I would not describe this grief recovery journey as one that is easy to recover from, I will use the word as a form of positive affirmation. I am able to recover. I am able to live through this. I can walk through the shadow of death. As David wrote, the Lord is with me.

Resilience indicates that I will bounce back. Sometimes I will have to remind myself that I can bounce back. There will be days when I will be down and won't feel like getting up. There will be days when I will want to pull the covers over my head and sleep the day away. However, resilience tells me that tomorrow will be better.

Come to think of it; my resilience is what has enabled me to write this book. It turns pain into purpose, and it has allowed me to be a blessing to others.

My mother was a very resilient woman. She endured and overcame so much, from colorism to domestic violence to racism. How could I not follow her example? Thank you, Lord, for my mother, who was a daily example of resilience. May I keep the faith and continue to recover.

Scripture

My soul is weary with sorrow; strengthen me according to your word.

~ **Psalm 119:28 NIV**

May our Lord Jesus Christ himself and God our Father, who loved us and by his grace gave us eternal encouragement and good hope, ^{17}encourage your hearts and strengthen you in every good deed and word.

~ **2 Thessalonians 2:16-17 NIV**

Prayer

Lord, while I am not fond of the way I am feeling right now, I also realize the foundation of my emotions is love. I sincerely loved my mother. Now, I sincerely miss her. I pray you infuse me with the spirit of resilience that she had so I can carry on in life lovingly and purposefully. In Jesus' name, I pray, Amen.

Embracing Your New Normal

Notes:

Race Run

As I read scripture during my devotions this morning, God ministered to me. Reading Hebrews 12 let me know we all have an earthly assignment or life's race to run. The thing is, none of us knows exactly when our race will conclude. For example, it would be great to know how long we have on this earth, be it 28, 50 or 67 years. Perhaps we would love harder, accomplish more, and be more determined to get things done within the allotted time given to us.

Alas, that is not the way this works. God does not provide end dates at the beginning of our lives. He does not provide them at all. At times this is frustrating because we are told to ask and we shall receive. As I think further, I realize that it is best for us that God not reveal how much time we have to run our races. Consider this. If we knew the date that our life's race would end, then we may decide to sit some laps out. We may opt to observe rather than participate. Someone would decide to jump in during the final year rather than remain consistent. We would undoubtedly miss some experiences and lessons that the Lord ordained to teach us, grow us, and ultimately bless us.

Also, God calls us to be at peace with each other. Peace is not a seasonal emotion. It is to be a permanent state. Therefore, consistent relationships are key. So, as we lament the unknown, I encourage you to act upon what is known. Let us love one another now while we are in the race. Let us practice patience and longsuffering now. Let's not delay implementing random acts of kindness, because tomorrow is not promised to anyone. We most likely will not reach the finish line at the same time. One will surely get there first, but as long as we stay the course, eventually we will hear the words, "well done."

Scripture

Do all that you can to live in peace with everyone.

~ Romans 12:18 NLT

Don't be selfish; don't try to impress others. Be humble, thinking of others as better than yourselves. [4]Don't look out only for your own interests, but take an interest in others, too.

~ Philippians 2:3-4 NLT

Prayer

Lord, sometimes I take time for granted. I forget that time is something that continues to move on with or without me. Forgive me for thinking that I have an unlimited supply of time. Forgive me for not prioritizing well. I pray over the areas where I have regrets. Father, help me to deal with them. Where possible, Lord, I ask you to help me redeem lost time. Help me to channel this emotion into a positive area. I do not want to become bitter but rather better. Help me, Lord. In your son Jesus' name, Amen.

Embracing Your New Normal

Notes:

_____
_____
_____
_____
_____
_____
_____
_____
_____
_____
_____
_____

Teraleen R. Campbell

Race Run, Part Two

Death means one's course has been concluded. They have reached the finish line; their race has ended. Yes, departure from Earth to glory denotes that their journey has been completed.

But wait, Lord! I wasn't ready for them to be finished! There was no real warning. I thought we were on this journey together. How could it be that they completed their race, but I was unaware they were nearing the end until after the fact? Yes, it's typical for children to bury their parents, but I still wasn't ready.

As I work through these thoughts, I realize that my mother's race was just that – her race. She did give me some indication that she was nearing the end two months prior to her passing, though. It was one of the most difficult days. I was informed she had decided to adjust her advance directive to DNR, which stands for do not resuscitate. My mother told me that she was getting tired, and if she coded, she was ready. She was confident that I would be alright. I stayed strong during the conversation. However, once outside in the parking lot, I lost it. I didn't even make it to my car before breaking down.

After my mother's passing, I started realizing that just as Cindy had run her race, I still have to run mine. Therefore, staying stuck in my grief was not an option. Part of that race involves this book and other books that I have written to encourage and uplift others. Imagine if I had not garnered the courage to revisit those emotions.

God continues giving me goals and dreams. Therefore, I must take steps to fulfill them, as they are stops along the path of my race. Every day, I steady myself and ask the Lord everyday to help me endure. I am reminded of the last verse of the hymn Hold to God's Unchanging Hand:

> *When your journey is completed,*
> *If to God you have been true,*
> *Fair and bright the home in glory*
> *Your enraptured soul will view.*

Scripture

Therefore, since we are surrounded by such a huge crowd of witnesses to the life of faith, let us strip off every weight that slows us down, especially the sin that so easily trips us up. And let us run with endurance the race God has set before us. [2]We do this by keeping our eyes on Jesus, the champion who initiates and perfects our faith. Because of the joy awaiting him, he endured the cross, disregarding its shame. Now he is seated in the place of honor beside God's throne. [3]Think of all the hostility he endured from sinful people; then you won't become weary and give up. [4]After all, you have not yet given your lives in your struggle against sin.

~ Hebrews 12:1-4 NLT

Prayer

Father, I thank you today for the gentle reminder that although I have lost people along this journey, I still have a race to run. I ask you to help me along the way. I acknowledge my frailties and ask you to give me strength on my weakest days. I also praise you for the assurance that those who have gone on before me have completed their course. I want to successfully do the same. In Jesus' name, I pray, Amen.

Embracing Your New Normal

Notes:

_____
_____
_____
_____
_____
_____
_____
_____
_____
_____
_____

I Didn't Know My Own Strength

This week marks one year since my mother went from Earth to glory. As I look back, I realize a great part of that first month was an absolute blur. I don't remember some of the specifics from Mom's funeral. I do, however, recall a church packed with three hundred or so people who braved the rain on the Saturday before Memorial Day to help me celebrate the life she had lived so valiantly.

I recall that the service was upbeat and joyful, just as she would have wanted it. I remember the tremendous outpour of love from my church family as well as my mother's church, and the support from the community was phenomenal.

Afterward, the business aspect set in. The week after the funeral, I returned to the nursing facility to retrieve all of my mother's belongings from her room. I bit the bullet and did it quickly for two reasons: 1) to get it over with and not procrastinate, and 2) to avoid charges from the facility.

Within one month, I received the death certificate. Then some documents needed to be signed, and important decisions needed to be made. Meanwhile, I continued to get mail with my mother's name on it as if she were still alive. It took everything within me to keep it together. The Lord reminded me that even when I can't trace Him, He would be there. I'm glad to say He has been faithful to His word.

As I look back over the past year, there were days when I was emotionally and physically spent as a result of grief. As a friend told me, grief is exhausting. I honestly do not know how I got the strength to make it, but I did. Then again, I know exactly where my strength came from – the Lord God Almighty. There were countless days when I did not feel as though I would make it, but just in the nick of time, God infused me with a strength that I didn't know I had. I am reminded of the song by the late, great Whitney Houston. She sang the words, "I didn't know my own strength." Whitney went on to proclaim, "I was not built to break."

She is absolutely right. I am Cindy Moses' (Cindy Mo's) daughter and a child of The Most High God. Therefore, I was not built to break.

Scripture
I look up to the mountains – does my help come from there? My help comes from the LORD, who made heaven and earth!
~ Psalm 121:1 NLT

Prayer
Thank you, Lord, for giving me strength that I did not know existed. Because of you, I have made it through, and I am very grateful. Amen!

Embracing Your New Normal

Notes:

Teraleen R. Campbell

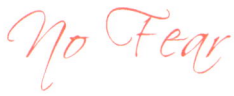

No Fear

The death of a loved one brings with it an entirely different and unwelcome emotion. That emotion is fear. Fear of the unknown – How will this void impact me? Fear due to the loss of income – How will I survive? Fear due to emotional loss – Who will love me now? Fear due to the void left after the physical loss of a loved one – Who will handle this role and these responsibilities?

Death can usher in the spirit of fear, if we allow it. Yes, we have the assurance that the person whom we lost has gone on to a better place, and we also feel a sense of relief that they are no longer in pain. However, we may still experience a level of fear. The emotion of fear is often not identified as a companion of grief. We do not realize that fear can be part of the grieving process, as well. Once we recognize this, we can deal with these uneasy and possibly previously unidentified feelings. Although it feels as though part of my heart has been ripped from my chest due to my loss, I can find solace in the words of John: Let not your heart be troubled. I will face my fears while also remembering the words of David from Psalm 27:1 and invoke them over my life: My heart will not fear.

I will give myself permission to be relieved of fear, understanding that God will still supply all of my needs. I am reminded of the Lion King's "Hakuna Matata," which means no worries. God's got me! He had me before, and He has me now!

Teraleen R. Campbell

Scripture

I am the true grapevine, and my Father is the gardener. ^{2}He cuts off every branch of mine that doesn't produce fruit, and he prunes the branches that do bear fruit so they will produce even more. ^{3}You have already been pruned and purified by the message I have given you. ^{4}Remain in me, and I will remain in you. For a branch cannot produce fruit if it is severed from the vine, and you cannot be fruitful unless you remain in me. ^{5}"Yes, I am the vine; you are the branches. Those who remain in me, and I in them, will produce much fruit. For apart from me you can do nothing.

~ **John 15:1-5 NLT**

Prayer

Father God, today I ask you to help me overcome the spirit of fear. In the name of Jesus, I cancel every type of fear. I abide in you, and in you, there is no fear. In you, there are no worries. I will emerge from this and produce fruit; I will be productive and not stagnant. This is my prayer. In Jesus' name, Amen!

Notes:

_____
_____
_____
_____
_____
_____
_____
_____
_____
_____
_____

Teraleen R. Campbell

A Day in the Pit

Today was one of those days when I can say that I really miss my mom. Beyond going to church, it has been a lonely day, and it made me wonder how many people would notice if I were no longer here. I wish my family were more connected than we are. Mind you, we don't have any hard feelings, but distance and age separate us.

Alas, I still have a life to live. I ask God for grace to run this race and to cover me. I do my best to move on and move forward. Even on this Easter Sunday, I am trying to get past the void that I am feeling. It hurts to think there is no dinner of ham, greens, and potato salad to take for her.

Today, I wore the same dress that I wore when I visited my mother on what turned out to be her final Easter on this earth. My sorority sister had made the trip with me to spend a few hours with her. Mom enjoyed the visit, but it was apparent she was not feeling well. While my sorority sister sang old hymns, Mom sang along with her. That's a day that I will never forget. As clear as it was that she wasn't well, she was able to muster up the strength to sing praises unto her God. Now, two years later, I feel as though I am praising Him from a dark place.

I miss you, Mommy, and I need the strength of the Lord to lift me.

Scripture

He gives power to the tired and worn out, and strength to the weak. ³⁰Even the youths shall be exhausted, and the young men will all give up. ³¹But they that wait upon the Lord shall renew their strength. They shall mount up with wings like eagles; they shall run and not be weary; they shall walk and not faint.

~ Isaiah 40:29-31 TLB

Prayer

Lord, I admit that I am not in the best place today. I need you to help me snap out of this. Your love and care for me remain unquestioned. I am simply having a human day. Help me through this. In Jesus' name, Amen.

Embracing Your New Normal

Notes:

_____
_____
_____
_____
_____
_____
_____
_____
_____
_____
_____
_____

Teraleen R. Campbell

I Still Give Thanks!

It's Thanksgiving Day. I've been so occupied with work and the release of my first solo book, that this week crept up on me. Of course, I experienced a moment of feeling melancholy this morning. I reflected on how much my mother and her sister, my aunt Josephine, loved this particular holiday. Both would do their share of the cooking. Mom would prepare the corn pudding, sweet potato pudding, green bean casserole, stuffing, and a few loaves of pumpkin bread, while Aunt Josephine would cook the turkey and the rest of the side dishes. Uncle Gandy always said grace before carving the turkey. In recent years, my aunt would tell Uncle Gandy to let me say Thanksgiving prayer, but I'd always defer to him. Truth be told, I love to hear a man pray.

Both my mother and aunt now rest with the angels. It's up to the next generation to maintain some level of togetherness and tradition. Cousin Tanny typically takes the lead on Thanksgiving dinner.

I haven't typically traveled on Thanksgiving Day for some time, but I would make sure Mom had a great meal. I'd wait until Saturday to see my family. Today one of my best friends and I went to a restaurant where they were serving Thanksgiving dinner. Afterward, we went to the mall. Our rationale? Walk off the food while getting in some retail therapy. Since I no longer buy a lot of gifts, today's outing was therapeutic. After dinner, shopping helped occupy our time and minds. At the end of the day, I can give thanks that Thanksgiving was bearable.

Scripture
Don't worry about anything; instead, pray about everything. Tell God what you need and thank him for all he has done.
~ Philippians 4:6 NLT

Prayer
Lord, I thank you for giving me ways to get through what I am going through. As I think of your goodness towards me and those connected to me, my heart remains full of gratefulness. I praise you not just today, but tomorrow and the next day because you are indeed worth it. Amen.

Embracing Your New Normal

Notes:

Teraleen R. Campbell

Help Yourself During the Holiday Season

The holidays are not always joyful for everyone. For some, such as myself, it will be the first Thanksgiving or Christmas since a loved one departed this earth. For others, the holiday season is a reminder of lost love due to a divorce or end of a relationship. Either way, separation anxiety is real and can be emotionally draining. Here are a few steps to help get you through the holiday season:

- Do not run from your emotions. Denial can be dangerous. Acknowledge your feelings but try not to get stuck in them.
- Take some time for yourself. Others may not understand, but you must do what is best for you, which includes getting proper rest.
- Refocus your energy. Volunteer for a charity or deliver holiday meals. Turn your loss into something positive that will uplift your spirits.
- In the case of death and grief, look for a way to honor the memory of your loved one. For example, my mother used to make pumpkin bread. Therefore, this year, I plan to make a loaf and take it to the office as a fond way to remember her.
- Journaling and capturing your feelings can be therapeutic as you work through your grief.
- Pray, pray, pray. In other words, tell God about it. Be

honest about how you are feeling. After all, He already knows. Release those feelings and emotions to the one who created you.

My prayer is although you may experience a wide range of emotions, you experience some level of peace, the type that surpasses even your human understanding.

Scripture
"Peace I leave with you; my peace I give to you. Not as the world gives do I give to you. Let not your hearts be troubled, neither let them be afraid."
~ John 14:27 ESV

And the peace of God, which surpasses all understanding, will guard your hearts and your minds in Christ Jesus.
~ Philippians 4:7 ESV

Prayer
Father, today I want to be completely honest with you about the way I am feeling. I need your help to get me through this season. I cast my cares upon you, and I receive the peace that only you can give. Thank you, Lord, in advance for peace!

Embracing Your New Normal

Notes:

Teraleen R. Campbell

Family Matters

There's a storm brewing within my family. That's not anything new, except this time, my mother is not here. I can't call her to talk it over. I can't seek her input and motherly wisdom. I can't ask her to pray that God will move in this situation.

Mom was one of the matriarchs of our family, although Aunt Josephine (my mother's sister) is 13 years older and outlived my mother. However, Cindy was known to be very approachable. She was also a great listener and gave good, sound advice without being judgmental. My mother demonstrated a balance between being practical and spiritual. Mom was also a woman of prayer and intercession, and she knew how to communicate well with others.

Since her transition, I feel as though I'm being pushed into a "keep-everyone-together" matriarch role, and quite honestly, I do not want it. I don't feel ready to fill my mother's shoes. I'm not even the oldest in the family. However, I seemingly am unable to avoid this. Help me, Lord!

Scripture

For everything there is a season, a time for every activity under heaven.

~ **Ecclesiastes 3:1 NLT**

For I can do everything through Christ, who gives me strength.

~ **Philippians 4:13 NLT**

Teraleen R. Campbell

Prayer

Father, today I am seeking your help in the hard place. I wholeheartedly believe and am aware that you have a plan for my family and me. I sense your plan includes a role that I am not comfortable with. However, as your servant, I recognize it is my duty to serve not only you but others, as well, including my family. I ask you to help me yield to your will and follow the leading of your spirit. I also pray that anger and bitterness do not overtake me. Let love continue to abide within the family. In Jesus' name, Amen!

Embracing Your New Normal

Notes:

_____
_____
_____
_____
_____
_____
_____
_____
_____
_____

Teraleen R. Campbell

Christmas

Less than two hours are remaining in this Christmas. Honestly, I had been dreading this day. A close friend and I discussed how we both were doing our best to cope by staying occupied. Alas, it hit me last night that Christmas Day's arrival was imminent; there was no way to escape it. I began to feel a seemingly uncontrollable level of anxiety. So, I went to bed early in hopes that I could avoid wallowing in sadness or sinking into an abyss.

This morning, I started the day with a serious cry at the thought that Christmas was my mother's favorite holiday; Thanksgiving was a close second. Mom loved helping young mothers and families during the holiday season. Seeing her bless so many others during my life motivated me to make Christmas special for her.

I cherished going home for Christmas, shopping as I prepared to do so, and ultimately watching as she opened her gifts. My goal was to see her happy on Christmas, and I kept that same drive even when she was in the nursing home.

This holiday season, I felt a sense of withdrawal. The main focus of my holiday is gone. What am supposed to do now? God, help me! I trust you and will praise you, even in this!

Scripture

The LORD is my strength and shield. I trust him with all my heart. He helps me, and my heart is filled with joy. I burst out in songs of thanksgiving.

~ Psalms 28:7 NLT

Those who live in the shelter of the Most High will find rest in the shadow of the Almighty. ²This I declare about the LORD: He alone is my refuge, my place of safety; he is my God, and I trust him.

~ Psalm 91:1-2 NLT

Prayer

Father, I pray for everyone faced with enduring a holiday without the earthly presence of a loved one. I ask that you surround them with love. I also ask that you guard them with the type of peace that will surpass even their understanding. Let it be so. In Jesus' name, Amen!

Embracing Your New Normal

Notes:

_____
_____
_____
_____
_____
_____
_____
_____
_____
_____

Teraleen R. Campbell

You Better Recognize

They say the first year is the hardest. I am not sure I believe that, because year one has come and gone. I do however, know I've been feeling some kind of way all week long. Do I like it? No. Have I tried to shake it? Yes. I have prayed, and I have read comforting and encouraging scriptures. Yes, they have been helpful, but they do not replace the void that I feel with missing my mommy.

I tried to go about my daily routine, but something seemed off. It was not anything external per se. Then, all of a sudden, grief hit me like a ton of bricks. I was emotionally down for the count and needed to regroup.

While I am still new at navigating this space, I do know it is important to recognize when you are not in a good head and heart space. It is necessary to allow yourself to feel whatever you are feeling, take whatever time you need, seek the Lord, and then move on. I have had to do this many times, without apology and without making a public announcement.

Everyone will not understand the way you are feeling, and that is perfectly fine. Remember, this is your grief recovery and life's journey. No two people's journey is the same. We love differently; therefore, we grieve differently.

Recognizing sometimes means you will need to seek outside support, such as a grief support group. It may also mean you need to obtain professional counseling. I have seen a therapist, who helped me put some things into perspective as it relates to my journey. She helped me recognize that within one year I had lost a close friend, my dog, and my mother. That realization helped me navigate the waters of grief differently.

You must do whatever is necessary to catch yourself before you get stuck. Don't be ashamed. God sends us help in various forms. Likewise, if you realize you are stuck in grief, you must seek help so you will ultimately be able to move forward, albeit taking baby steps. Once you recognize where you are, then you can make adjustments that are necessary to move forward.

Scripture

When you go through deep waters, I will be with you. When you go through rivers of difficulty, you will not drown. When you walk through the fire of oppression, you will not be burned up; the flames will not consume you. ³For I am the LORD, your God, the Holy One of Israel, your Savior.

~ Isaiah 43:2-3 NLT

Prayer

Heavenly Father, although I'm not feeling the best right now, I give you praise. First, I praise you for the ability to recognize that I am not up to par. Second, I praise you because I know this too shall pass. I thank you in advance for helping me to regroup and recover. While every day is different, you, God, are constant. I speak now that I lack nothing, even at this point in my life. This is my prayer and affirmation today. In Jesus' name, Amen!

Embracing Your New Normal

Notes:

Bonus Chapters

Change

People say one changes after the death of a parent or spouse. I can confirm that the statement is indeed true. Adapting to the change that has occurred is the essence of accepting a new normal. After enduring the worst aspect of a life-changing situation, it makes perfect sense for there to be some positive outcomes. Living through loss causes us to view things differently. For example, I recall regular trips to Ruby Tuesday and ordering the strawberry tall cake with one of my best friends. After her sudden death, I no longer view that restaurant in the same light. I very rarely go there because the experience is now different.

After becoming my mother's caregiver, I gained an increased awareness of the importance of remaining healthy. While I have long struggled with my weight, I became more focused on eating healthier and becoming more active. I completed my first 10K walk during this time. I also learned a new term – self-care.

I became intentional in taking better care of myself. At that time, it was because I knew my mother needed me to be there for her. After she passed, I admit I fell off while immersed in grief. However, I realized I had to develop a healthier lifestyle because my own life depended on it.

As we work to navigate the changes that have come upon us as a result of death, I offer a few suggestions that will assist with actualizing positive outcomes. Ask the Lord to help you implement them.

- Create new traditions
- Tackle your life's goals. Recognize you may not have as much time as you think
- Evaluate your priorities
- Check your squad/inner circle
- Participate in activities that will honor the memory of the dearly departed

Scripture

"For I know the plans I have for you," declares the LORD, "plans to prosper you and not to harm you, plans to give you hope and a future."

~ **Jeremiah 29:11 NIV**

The LORD himself goes before you and will be with you; he will never leave you nor forsake you. Do not be afraid; do not be discouraged.

~ **Deuteronomy 31:8 NIV**

Prayer

Dear Lord, I admit that I am a creature of habit. Therefore, accepting and adjusting to change is challenging. I really do need you to help me at this stage in my life. I realize that your word says that you will go before me and prepare the way, and I am so grateful. I am most thankful to know that despite earthly death, you remain with me. This knowledge enables me to go forth with my life in your strength and power. My hope and trust indeed are in you, Oh Lord. Amen.

Notes:

Not a Day Goes By

Although we didn't speak every day, now that you're gone, I miss you daily. We shared a bond like no other. Not a single day goes by that I don't miss you, Mommy. Sometimes those thoughts originate from minuscule circumstances – a song, a situation, a smile.

Every time your beloved Washington Redskins are mentioned during football season, I think of you. I used to enter the month of March with enthusiasm because it was your birthday. I looked forward to celebrating you and making sure you knew how much you were loved. Now I feel some kind of way because you are not here. Many of your characteristics come to mind regularly:

- Your drive to overcome life's obstacles
- Your loving yet no-nonsense nature
- Your passion for prayer
- Your ability to meet people where they are rather than condemn them
- The way you mentored so many younger women
- Your unwavering love for God and commitment to serving the Lord and others
- Your favorite crab cakes and the days when you sent me to KFC for chicken
- Your love for dogs
- The way you went out of your way to make sure single

mothers could provide a decent Thanksgiving and Christmas for their children
- ➤ Your keen sense of fashion and style, including your love of hats

Thankfully, I have these and other fond memories to lift me, even when they come along with tears. Sometimes I make pumpkin bread or corn pudding simply because the family loved it when you made them for holiday gatherings. I am extremely grateful to have been birthed by a woman who meant so much not only to me but to others, as well. I am thinking of you with love.

Scripture
And now, dear brothers and sisters, one final thing. Fix your thoughts on what is true, and honorable, and right, and pure, and lovely, and admirable. Think about things that are excellent and worthy of praise. [9]Keep putting into practice all you learned and received from me—everything you heard from me and saw me doing. Then the God of peace will be with you.
~ Philippians 4:8-9 NLT

Prayer
Dear Lord, today I thank you for the memories. I appreciate every memory because they represent the positive interactions that we have shared. I ask that the memories be a source of strength and not lead to depression. I honor you and the memory of all whom I have loved but are now departed. Amen.

Embracing Your New Normal

Notes:

_____
_____
_____
_____
_____
_____
_____
_____
_____
_____
_____

Teraleen R. Campbell

Final Thoughts

Perhaps you did not enjoy a close relationship with your parent, or perhaps they were taken from this earth too soon and you did not have the opportunity to bond with them and missed making memories. Perhaps you were estranged from them. Whatever the situation, the finality of death leaves a sting that is unmentionable, indescribable, and cannot be articulated adequately. In most cases, it feels unbearable.

All of that being the case, please know that you are in my thoughts and prayers. You can make it. We will get through. We can and will move forward. It is challenging, but we will do it - one day at a time, one hour at a time, one moment at a time. Yes, we can with the Lord as our helper. We will keep living.

Parting Words of Prayer

Seal and cover the reader. Help them to embrace that which is new and uncomfortable.

Father, even now in the name of the Lord Jesus, I pray that the strength of those who have read this book has been multiplied with the turning of each page. I pray that they have been encouraged in knowing that they are not alone in their quest to accept and embrace this new normal in their life.

I pray that grief does not overtake them to the point that it results in mental or physical illness. I ask You to help them find joy, comfort, and peace in the memories of their loved one. Lord, help each reader to reconcile the difficult circumstances surrounding death itself. Circumstances vary, and we know that this is never easy, but with Your help, we can find peace and deal with this change. Lord, where there are questions that remain unanswered, I ask You to help Your people to reconcile. I pray that Your healing virtue would permeate their atmosphere.

You are our God, our strength, and our helper. We look to You. We need You to establish a new order in our lives. We come to You because we can only count on You to help us with this. This is our prayer. In Jesus' name, Amen!

To my Heavenly Father: thank you so much for loving me and for choosing me for this great work. I love you, Lord!

To my family: we have encountered so much change over the past three years, but we are still standing. I love you all!

To friends who are like family: Please know that I appreciate every time you traveled up the road with me or to support me, every gift, every meal you prepared or purchased, every prayer you prayed, and every time you lent a listening ear.

To my Greater Mount Calvary Holy Church and King's Apostle Church families, Dr. Mary Breaux Wright, and my Zeta Phi Beta Sorors: thank you for every prayer you prayed, every card, every text message, every social media post, every word of encouragement, and every kind sentiment. They helped keep me on my feet when my strength was weak.

To everyone who encouraged and nudged me to write this book: I thank you for pushing me so that I can help others.

To Charron Monaye and the Pen Legacy Publishing Family: thank you for all that you have done to help me share this message.

To everyone who encouraged and supported me as I worked to fulfill this God-given assignment, thank you.

About the Author

Teraleen R. Campbell is a native of Hagerstown, Maryland, and currently resides in the Washington, DC metropolitan area. She is an award-winning author and speaker. In addition to serving in the ministry, she is a certified coach. One who knows the worth of prayer, Teraleen loves to intercede for others. She serves as lead intercessor each month for the Sisters Prayer Circle, which is sponsored by Sisters 4 Sisters, Inc.

She became a member of Zeta Phi Beta Sorority, Inc. at the University of Maryland, where she conducted her undergraduate studies. She has numerous leadership positions in the organization, previously serving as National Co-Director of Marketing. Her ministry extends to Zeta, as she now serves on the International Interfaith Team. Teraleen authored the sorority's Centennial Prayer, has facilitated the Global Day of Prayer, and co-authored the Faith of Our Founders Devotional Book.

Her community involvement includes the Prince George's County March for Babies Committee and Maryland Legislative Agenda for Women. She is Immediate Past President of a local club for Toastmasters International. Teraleen is a tireless advocate against domestic violence, engaging elected officials, supporting survivors, conducting workshops, and sitting on panels that address this issue.

Southern Management Corporation, the March of Dimes, and the American Red Cross have recognized her for her involvement and service to the community. Additionally, she was named Sorority Woman of the Year during the annual Sister-to-Sister Sorority Luncheon hosted by Taylor Thomas of WHUR Radio. She also was recognized by her sorority, having been inducted into Zeta's Maryland State Hall of Fame in 2016. She was named one of the DC Metropolitan area's 100 Phenomenal Women in 2015. She is a contributing author of *Behind the Scenes of a Phenomenal Woman* and *Confessions of a Caregiver,* which were released in 2018 and 2019.

With Christ as her focus, friend, and guide, Minister Campbell's earnest desire is to be a vessel fit for the Master's use. (2 Timothy 2:21)

Check Out Other Books Authored & Co-Authored by Teraleen Campbell

www.ingramcontent.com/pod-product-compliance
Lightning Source LLC
Chambersburg PA
CBHW042116100526
44587CB00025B/4083